BREAKING THE GROWTH BARRIER

Transforming Your Business into a Market Leader

SUMAN RANGABHASHYAM

Qurate
quratebooks.com

Book Creation Services

by

BookMyStory

It's time to tell your story

www.bookmystorypublishing.com

A venture of

R&S Enterprises

BREAKING THE GROWTH BARRIER

Transforming Your Business into a Market Leader

Suman Rangabhashyam

Published by Qurate Books Pvt. Ltd.

Published in 2023

ISBN: 978-93-5898-107-0

Qurate
quratebooks.com

Qurate Books Pvt. Ltd.
Goa 403523, India
www.quratebooks.com
Tel: 1800-210-6527, Email: info@quratebooks.com

PREFACE

Dear Reader,

Welcome to "Breaking the Growth Barrier: A Guide for Budding Visionaries." I am thrilled to embark on this journey with you as we delve into the dynamic world of entrepreneurship, where dreams are transformed into reality, and innovation knows no bounds.

This book is born out of a deep passion for entrepreneurship, a fervent belief in the power of ideas, and a commitment to nurturing the spirit of innovation that resides within each one of us. Over the years, I have witnessed countless individuals embark on the exhilarating, yet often challenging, path of entrepreneurship. Some have soared to great heights, while others have encountered unexpected obstacles. Through their stories and my own experiences, I have come to understand that entrepreneurship is not just a career choice; it's a way of life.

"Breaking the Growth Barrier " is designed to be your trusted companion on this remarkable journey. Whether you're a first-time entrepreneur with a world-changing idea, a seasoned business owner looking to innovate, or simply someone who dreams of turning their passion into a profession, this book is for you. Its pages are filled with wisdom, strategies, and practical advice that will help you navigate the complex landscape of entrepreneurship.

In the pages that follow, we will explore the fundamental principles of entrepreneurship, from conceiving a compelling vision to building a resilient business model. We will delve into the art of identifying market opportunities, understanding your target audience, and crafting a powerful brand. You will learn how to develop a growth mindset, embrace failure as a stepping stone to success, and harness the invaluable resource of resilience.

But this book is not just about theory; it's a hands-on guide that provides real-world examples, case studies, and actionable steps. It's about rolling up your sleeves, taking risks, and putting your ideas into motion. It's about fostering a spirit of creativity, adaptability, and continuous learning, which are the cornerstones of successful entrepreneurship.

Throughout these pages, you will find stories of entrepreneurs who started with nothing but an idea and turned it into a thriving business. Their journeys are filled with highs and lows, setbacks and triumphs, and invaluable lessons that will inspire and inform your own entrepreneurial adventure.

As you embark on this quest, remember that entrepreneurship is not a destination but a journey, one that will test your resolve, stretch your limits, and reward your persistence. Embrace the uncertainty, celebrate the victories, and learn from the challenges. And most importantly, never lose sight of the impact you can have on the world through your innovation, dedication, and passion.

I am honoured to be your guide on this transformative voyage. So, let's set sail together into the boundless sea of entrepreneurship, where opportunities await those who dare to dream, create, and lead. May this book serve as a beacon of inspiration, knowledge, and empowerment as you unleash your entrepreneurial spirit and embark on a path of limitless possibility.

With enthusiasm and anticipation,

Suman Rangabhashyam

CONTENTS

CHAPTER 1

Unveiling the Top Challenges of Entrepreneurs Pursuing Exponential Growth

An entrepreneur tends to bite off a little more than he can chew hoping he'll quickly learn how to chew it. - ROY ASH

Welcome, fellow entrepreneurs, to a chapter dedicated to the exciting and sometimes daunting challenges that await those seeking exponential business growth in the vibrant Indian market. As you embark on this thrilling journey, it's crucial to be aware of the unique hurdles you may encounter.

Here are some of the conversations I hear as a Financial Business Coach from entrepreneurs across the world.

Picture this: I've got this grand vision for explosive growth, but guess what? It's like trying to paint a masterpiece with a tiny brush and limited colours. My budget is tighter than a clenched fist, finding skilled talent feels like a treasure hunt, and the cutting-edge technology I need is playing hard to get.

let's talk about the dance of competition in the Indian market. It's like entering a dazzling ballroom filled with top-notch dancers, each showcasing their moves. It's a fierce battle for attention. But you know what? I've got my dancing shoes on, and I'm ready to break some moves that no one has seen before. I'm infusing my business with a unique flavour, adding a dash of desi spice to stand out."

1. The Great Resource Conundrum:

Visualize this: You have an audacious vision, a burning desire for growth, but limited resources to make it happen. Be it financial constraints, a lack of skilled manpower, or limited access to advanced technology, resource scarcity can feel like a giant roadblock. But fear not! In the land of jugaad, where innovation thrives, entrepreneurs have mastered the art of doing more with less.

2. The Dance of Competition:

Ah, competition! It's like a thrilling dance that keeps you on your toes. In India's bustling marketplace, you'll encounter rivals, both established industry giants and ambitious startups, all vying for their slice of the pie. But fret not, my entrepreneurial friend. This competitive landscape ignites the fire of innovation within us, pushing us to create unique value propositions and win the hearts of our customers.

3. The Maze of Market Uncertainty:

The Indian market is like a thrilling rollercoaster ride, with twists and turns that keep you guessing. Economic fluctuations, ever-changing consumer preferences, and unpredictable market trends make it a maze to navigate. But guess what? With a dash of resilience, adaptability, and a keen eye for emerging opportunities, you can ride this rollercoaster to exponential growth.

4. Marketing Mayhem:

Imagine standing in a crowded bazaar, vying for attention amid the chaos. Welcome to the world of customer acquisition in India! Crafting effective marketing strategies, building a strong brand presence, generating leads, and nurturing customer relationships can feel like a whirlwind. But fear not, for in the land of diversity and ingenuity, creative marketing tactics can set you apart from the crowd.

5. Scaling Everest:

Scaling your business is like climbing Mount Everest—challenging yet exhilarating. As you ascend the heights of growth, you'll face the complexities of expanding operations while maintaining quality, efficiency, and customer satisfaction. Streamlining logistics, optimizing supply chains, hiring the right talent, and refining processes are the tools you'll need to conquer this summit.

6. The Cash Flow Tango:

In the dance of business, cash flow management takes centre stage. With delayed payments, unexpected expenses, and the constant need for financing, entrepreneurs in India face unique challenges. But fear not, for here, resourcefulness and innovative financial strategies come to your rescue, enabling you to keep the cash flow tango alive and thriving.

7. The Quest for Talent:

Finding the right talent to fuel your growth can be like searching for the legendary philosopher's stone. In India's competitive job market, attracting and retaining skilled employees is a challenge.

But don't lose heart! Create a work culture that fosters growth, offers exciting opportunities, and nurtures talent. Remember, the right people can be the catalyst for exponential success.

8. The Innovation Odyssey:

Innovation is the heartbeat of India's entrepreneurial ecosystem. But with rapidly advancing technology and evolving customer needs, staying ahead requires an innovation odyssey. Balancing the need for disruptive ideas while maintaining operational stability is a tightrope walk. Embrace the spirit of jugaad, foster a culture of creativity, and watch as your business transforms through innovation.

9. The Time Management Symphony:

As an entrepreneur, time is your most precious resource. With endless tasks, meetings, and deadlines, managing time effectively can seem like a symphony that needs perfect orchestration. Embrace productivity hacks, prioritize tasks wisely, and empower yourself with effective delegation to create harmony in your entrepreneurial journey.

10. The Legal Labyrinth:

Legal compliance may feel like navigating a labyrinth, with its complex regulations and compliance requirements. Tax laws, industry-specific regulations, intellectual property protection—all can be overwhelming. But remember, in India, resilience and the ability to navigate through the legal maze are key. Seek expert guidance, stay updated, and ensure your business sails smoothly through legal waters.

In this chapter, we embarked on a journey through the captivating challenges that entrepreneurs face while pursuing exponential growth in the Indian context. From limited resources to fierce competition, from market uncertainties to talent quests, each challenge is an opportunity for growth and learning. So, fellow entrepreneurs, embrace the uniqueness of the Indian landscape, fuel your passion with the spirit of jugaad, and march forward fearlessly on your path to exponential success. Stay tuned as we delve deeper into each challenge in the chapters ahead, providing you with valuable insights, practical strategies, and inspiring stories from fellow Indian entrepreneurs. Together, let's conquer the challenges and script remarkable growth stories.

CHAPTER 2

Unveiling the Desires of Entrepreneurs

"An entrepreneur's desires are the whispers of a future they're committed to creating."

In the bustling city of Hyderabad, where tradition and technology intertwine seamlessly, I found myself immersed in a captivating encounter that would shed light on the deepest desires of entrepreneurs. As the sun dipped below the horizon, casting a golden glow over the iconic Charminar, I sat in a cosy café eagerly awaiting the arrival of Vivek, the owner of a digital marketing development company.

Vivek, a visionary entrepreneur, walked in with an air of determination, his eyes lit up with a flicker of hope amidst the challenges he faced. Six years ago, he had embarked on his entrepreneurial journey, fuelled by a passion for innovation and a hunger for success. In those early years, his business soared, riding the crest of the digital revolution that swept across the city.

However, as the years passed, the once rapid growth began to slow, leaving Vivek searching for answers.

As we settled in, the aroma of freshly brewed Irani chai mingled with the chatter of fellow entrepreneurs sharing their stories of triumph and struggle. Vivek's eyes met mine, brimming with anticipation, as he began to unravel his desires, hoping that I could provide the guidance he sought to reignite the flame of exponential growth.

Desire 1: Reigniting the Passionate Flame

Vivek longed to rekindle the passionate flame that had fuelled his entrepreneurial spirit in the early days. The days when every new client brought an exhilarating surge of energy, and every innovative idea felt like a stroke of genius. He yearned to recapture that contagious enthusiasm that had once driven his business forward, infusing every project with boundless creativity and unwavering dedication.

Desire 2: Unlocking the Gates of Innovation

The second desire burning within Vivek's heart was an unquenchable thirst for innovation. He had witnessed first-hand the transformative power of disruptive ideas and ground-breaking solutions that had propelled his competitors to great heights. Vivek dreamed of being at the forefront of innovation, of creating products and services that would captivate his target audience and set new industry benchmarks. He yearned to forge a path of innovation that would leave a lasting impact on the ever-evolving landscape of Hyderabad's digital realm.

Desire 3: Scaling the Summit of Success

Vivek's eyes gleamed with determination as he shared his third desire—a burning ambition to scale the summit of success. Hyderabad, with its vibrant start-up ecosystem and burgeoning entrepreneurial spirit, beckoned him to expand his business beyond its current boundaries. He envisioned his company spreading its wings across the city, then the state, and eventually making its mark on the national stage. Vivek longed to be recognized as a force to be reckoned with, a pioneer in his field, and a catalyst for change in the business landscape of Hyderabad.

Desire 4: Building a Tribe of Loyal Customers

With a mix of yearning and frustration, Vivek expressed his desire to build a tribe of loyal customers who would rally behind his brand. He longed to create a community that resonated with his company's values—a community that would not just be customers but passionate advocates, singing praises of his brand from every corner of Hyderabad. Vivek yearned to forge deep connections, foster unwavering support, and earn the trust of his customers that would transcend transactions and transform them into loyal, lifelong partners.

Desire 5: Achieving a Balanced Entrepreneurial Life

Amidst the frenetic pace of entrepreneurship, Vivek shared his heartfelt desire for a balanced life. He yearned for a harmonious blend of his professional pursuits and personal well-being—a life where he could dedicate quality time to his loved ones, nurture his passions outside of work, and experience the joys that lie beyond the realm of his business. Vivek longed for a life that would bring fulfilment not just as an entrepreneur, but also as a family member, friend, and individual.

As Vivek's desires unfolded against the backdrop of Hyderabad's rich tapestry of culture, innovation, and aspirations, I couldn't help but be captivated by the shared aspirations of entrepreneurs. These desires were not mere whims or fleeting fantasies; they were the driving forces behind their tireless pursuit of growth and success. And in that moment, I felt the weight of responsibility resting upon my shoulders—to guide Vivek and countless other entrepreneurs on their quest to transform these desires into tangible reality.

Join me as we dive deeper into each of these desires, exploring the strategies, insights, and transformative actions that can pave the way to exponential business growth. Together, we shall embark on a transformative journey, empowering entrepreneurs like Vivek to achieve their dreams, conquer challenges, and embrace a future where their desires are fulfilled amidst the vibrant cityscape of Hyderabad.

CHAPTER 3

Mindset

"Mind is a flexible mirror, adjust it, to see a better world." — Amit Ray.

MINDSET: Mindset plays a pivotal role in the quest for exponential business growth. It is the foundation upon which entrepreneurs build their strategies, make decisions, and navigate the challenges that come their way. A growth mindset, in particular, can be a powerful catalyst that propels entrepreneurs toward extraordinary success.

A growth mindset is characterized by a belief that abilities and intelligence can be developed through dedication, effort, and learning. Entrepreneurs with a growth mindset embrace challenges as opportunities for growth, persist in the face of setbacks, seek out feedback and learning experiences, and view the success of others as inspiration rather than threats. This mindset empowers entrepreneurs to continually expand their skills, knowledge, and capabilities, enabling them to adapt, innovate, and seize opportunities for exponential business growth.

With a growth mindset, entrepreneurs embrace failure as a stepping stone to success. They understand that setbacks and obstacles are not permanent roadblocks but valuable lessons that provide insights for improvement and growth. Rather than being discouraged by failures, they learn from them, adjust their strategies, and approach challenges with renewed vigour.

Moreover, a growth mindset fuels entrepreneurs with a relentless drive for learning and self-improvement. They actively seek out new knowledge, acquire relevant skills, and stay updated with the latest industry trends. They surround themselves with mentors, advisors, and a network of like-minded individuals who inspire and challenge them to push beyond their limits.

Entrepreneurs with a growth mindset also foster a culture of innovation within their organizations. They encourage their teams to think creatively, take calculated risks, and embrace change. They understand that innovation is the lifeblood of exponential growth and continuously explore new ways to disrupt the market, differentiate their offerings, and meet evolving customer needs.

Crucially, a growth mindset instils resilience and determination within entrepreneurs. They understand that success is not an overnight phenomenon but a result of consistent effort, perseverance, and a willingness to adapt. They view challenges as opportunities for personal and professional growth, and setbacks as temporary detours on the path to success.

In conclusion, a growth mindset is a potent tool for entrepreneurs seeking exponential business growth. It empowers them to embrace challenges, learn from failures, foster innovation, and persist in the face of adversity. By cultivating a growth mindset, entrepreneurs can unlock their full potential, propel their businesses to new heights, and embark on a journey of continuous growth and success.

(1) PRODUCT / SERVICE:

Picture this: You have a brilliant idea for a product that has the potential to revolutionize the market. It's innovative, unique, and fills a gap that no other product can. But how can this product help entrepreneurs achieve exponential business growth? Let's explore the exciting possibilities.

First and foremost, a remarkable product sets the stage for differentiation. In a crowded marketplace, standing out is crucial. Your product, with its exceptional features and benefits, captures the attention of customers, making them curious and eager to explore what you have to offer. This curiosity can quickly turn into excitement, driving word-of-mouth referrals and generating a buzz around your brand.

Moreover, a truly remarkable product becomes an invaluable marketing tool. Entrepreneurs can leverage its distinctiveness to create compelling stories that resonate with their target audience. A captivating narrative combined with an extraordinary product creates an emotional connection, inspiring customers to not just buy the product, but become advocates for it. These brand ambassadors spread the word, attracting more customers and expanding your reach exponentially.

Furthermore, a great product cultivates customer loyalty. When customers experience the remarkable benefits your product provides, they develop a deep sense of trust and satisfaction. They become repeat buyers, creating a steady stream of revenue. But it doesn't end there. Satisfied customers are more likely to become brand advocates, sharing their positive experiences on social media, writing glowing reviews, and referring their friends and family. This organic growth is the fuel that drives exponential business growth.

A standout product also attracts strategic partnerships and collaborations. When other businesses see the value and potential in your product, they're eager to join forces. Partnerships can open doors to new markets, provide access to resources, and amplify your reach. This collaborative approach accelerates growth by leveraging the expertise and networks of like-minded entrepreneurs who share your vision.

Lastly, a remarkable product fuels innovation and continuous improvement. As entrepreneurs, we should never settle for mediocrity. By embracing customer feedback, staying attuned to market trends, and investing in research and development, we can enhance our product to stay ahead of the competition. This commitment to innovation ensures that our business remains at the forefront of the industry, constantly evolving and attracting new customers while delighting our existing ones.

In conclusion, a remarkable product serves as a catalyst for exponential business growth. It differentiates you from the competition, fuels word-of-mouth marketing, cultivates customer loyalty, attracts strategic partnerships, and drives a culture of innovation. So, unleash your creativity, develop a product that captures the imagination, and watch as your business soars to new heights, propelled by the power of an extraordinary product.

(2) USP :

Imagine stepping into a marketplace bustling with competitors vying for the attention of customers. How can entrepreneurs stand out and achieve exponential business growth amidst this sea of noise? The answer lies in crafting a unique selling proposition (USP) that captivates and compels. Let's dive into the captivating world of USPs and discover their potential to drive exponential business growth.

A USP is like a secret weapon that entrepreneurs wield to carve out a distinct space in the market. It is the essence of what sets your business apart from others and makes it irresistible to customers. A well-crafted USP grabs attention, piques curiosity, and creates a lasting impression.

The power of a compelling USP lies in its ability to clearly communicate the unique value that your product or service brings to the table. It goes beyond simply highlighting features; it taps into the deeper needs and desires of your target audience. By articulating a compelling promise or solving a pressing problem, your USP becomes the beacon that attracts customers who resonate with your offering.

Think of successful companies like Apple or Nike—brands that have harnessed the power of a strong USP. Apple's USP revolves around innovation, simplicity, and design, while Nike's USP is rooted in empowerment and inspiration. These companies have crafted USPs that resonate deeply with their target audience, forging emotional connections and fostering brand loyalty.

A captivating USP also helps entrepreneurs establish a unique positioning in the market. By identifying a specific niche or target market, entrepreneurs can tailor their messaging and offerings to cater to the unique needs and preferences of their customers. This targeted approach allows entrepreneurs to become the go-to solution for a specific segment, positioning themselves as the experts in that particular area.

Additionally, a well-defined USP enhances brand recognition and recall. When customers encounter a product or service that aligns with their needs and desires, and that stands out from the crowd, they are more likely to remember and recommend it to others. This organic word-of-mouth promotion can snowball, creating a ripple effect that fuels exponential growth.

Furthermore, a compelling USP provides entrepreneurs with a strategic advantage when it comes to pricing. By differentiating your offering through a unique value proposition, you can command a premium price, as customers perceive your product or service to be worth the investment. This, in turn, boosts profitability and creates a solid foundation for sustained growth.

In conclusion, a captivating USP is a game-changer for entrepreneurs seeking exponential business growth. It enables you to cut through the noise, connect with your target audience on a deeper level, establish a unique positioning, and command a premium in the market. So, harness the power of a well-crafted USP, infuse it with creativity and authenticity, and watch as your business rises above the competition, propelled by the irresistible allure of a unique selling proposition.

(3) MOTIVATED TEAM:

In the vast landscape of entrepreneurship, the value of a motivated team cannot be overstated. They are the driving force behind exponential business growth, propelling entrepreneurs to reach new heights. Let's embark on a captivating journey to explore how building a motivated team can ignite the spark of success and fuel exponential growth.

A motivated team is a powerhouse of creativity, innovation, and productivity. When team members are passionate about their work, they go above and beyond, bringing fresh perspectives and ideas to the table. They become intrinsically invested in the success of the business, going the extra mile to deliver exceptional results. This collective drive for excellence becomes the foundation upon which exponential growth is built.

A motivated team fosters a culture of collaboration and synergy. When team members are inspired and motivated, they willingly share their expertise, support one another, and work together towards common goals. This collaboration leads to the seamless flow of ideas, efficient problem-solving, and a collective drive to overcome challenges. The sum becomes greater than its parts, and the business gains a competitive edge in the market.

Moreover, a motivated team acts as brand ambassadors. They embody the values and vision of the entrepreneur, radiating enthusiasm and passion for the business. Whether interacting with clients, partners, or the wider community, their genuine enthusiasm leaves a lasting impression. This positive representation elevates the brand's reputation, attracts new opportunities, and cultivates strong, long-lasting relationships—key ingredients for exponential growth.

A motivated team also nurtures an environment of continuous learning and growth. They embrace opportunities for professional development, seek out new skills, and stay abreast of industry trends. This thirst for knowledge translates into enhanced expertise, enabling the business to stay ahead of the curve and seize emerging opportunities. As the team evolves and expands its capabilities, the business can scale and diversify, opening doors to exponential growth.

Furthermore, a motivated team fuels innovation and adaptability. When team members are encouraged to think creatively, take risks, and challenge the status quo, they become catalysts for change. Their fresh ideas and perspectives drive innovation within the organization, leading to the development of groundbreaking products, services, and processes. This ability to adapt and innovate fuels exponential growth in an ever-evolving business landscape.

Lastly, a motivated team enhances employee retention and attracts top talent. When team members feel valued, recognized, and motivated, they are more likely to stay committed to the business. This continuity allows for the accumulation of knowledge, expertise, and strong team dynamics. Additionally, a motivated team creates a magnetic pull, attracting high-performing individuals who are inspired by the positive work culture and the potential for exponential growth.

In conclusion, building a motivated team is a cornerstone of entrepreneurial success and exponential business growth. It fosters creativity, collaboration, and a shared sense of purpose. A motivated team becomes the driving force behind innovation, brand advocacy, and continuous learning. So, invest in your team, cultivate their motivation, and witness the transformative power of a motivated team as it propels your business towards exponential growth, leaving a trail of success in its wake.

(4) CUSTOMER CENTRIC :

Imagine a world where entrepreneurs have an unwavering focus on their customers—a world where businesses are built around understanding and fulfilling the needs of their target audience. In this captivating realm, a customer-centric approach becomes the catalyst for exponential business growth. Let's embark on a journey to explore how putting customers at the heart of your business can unlock extraordinary success.

A customer-centric approach creates a deep connection with your target audience. By truly understanding their needs, desires, and pain points, entrepreneurs can develop products and services that resonate on a profound level. This empathetic understanding creates a sense of trust, loyalty, and emotional attachment, turning customers into passionate advocates who eagerly share their positive experiences and attract new customers. This organic word-of-mouth promotion becomes the fuel that drives exponential growth.

Moreover, a customer-centric approach fuels innovation and continuous improvement. By listening to customer feedback, entrepreneurs gain valuable insights that drive product development and service enhancements. This iterative process ensures that businesses are constantly evolving to meet the evolving needs of their customers. As a result, entrepreneurs can stay ahead of the competition, capture emerging trends, and seize new opportunities for growth.

A customer-centric approach also fosters long-term relationships. By going above and beyond to exceed customer expectations, entrepreneurs create an unparalleled customer experience that sets them apart from their competitors. This exceptional experience builds trust, loyalty, and a sense of community. Customers become more than just transactions; they become valued partners in the business journey, providing valuable feedback, referrals, and even co-creating new offerings. These long-term relationships become a solid foundation for sustained growth.

Additionally, a customer-centric approach drives brand differentiation. In a crowded marketplace, businesses that truly understand and cater to their customers' unique needs stand out. By tailoring products, services, and marketing messages to resonate with specific customer segments, entrepreneurs can position themselves as the go-to solution for their target audience. This differentiation creates a competitive advantage that attracts customers and drives exponential growth.

Furthermore, a customer-centric approach enables entrepreneurs to anticipate and adapt to changing market dynamics. By staying closely connected to their customers, entrepreneurs can detect shifts in preferences, emerging trends, and new opportunities. This agility allows businesses to pivot, innovate, and capture new markets, driving exponential growth in the face of evolving customer demands.

In conclusion, a customer-centric approach is the cornerstone of exponential business growth. By deeply understanding and fulfilling the needs of your customers, you create powerful emotional connections, foster innovation, build long-term relationships, differentiate your brand, and adapt to changing market dynamics. So, immerse yourself in the world of your customers, embrace their perspectives, and let their needs guide your journey towards extraordinary success and exponential growth.

CHAPTER 4

Embracing Responsibility: Fuelling Exponential Business Growth

"The biggest risk is not taking any risk. In a world that's changing quickly, the only strategy that is guaranteed to fail is not taking risks."

- Mark Zuckerberg

Responsibility is the cornerstone of sustainable success and exponential business growth. In this chapter, we will explore the vital role of responsibility in the entrepreneurial journey. By understanding and embracing responsibility, entrepreneurs can create a strong foundation for their businesses to thrive. We will delve into the various aspects of responsibility, from leadership and customer focus to employee well-being and societal impact. Let us embark on this transformative journey toward a more responsible and prosperous entrepreneurial path.

The Entrepreneur's Role as a Responsible Leader:

As an entrepreneur, your role as a leader is pivotal in shaping the culture of your organization. Embodying responsibility means setting high ethical standards, leading by example, and fostering a culture of accountability within your team. Your leadership is instrumental in driving exponential growth by inspiring and empowering your team members to act responsibly and align their actions with the company's values.

Responsibility to Customers and Clients:

Building strong relationships with customers and clients requires a deep sense of responsibility. By consistently delivering value, ensuring product/service quality, and fostering transparent communication, you can build trust and loyalty. Going the extra mile to exceed customer expectations creates a competitive advantage and drives exponential growth through positive word-of-mouth and customer advocacy.

Responsibility to Employees and Team Members:

Your team is the lifeblood of your business, and their well-being and development should be a top priority. Creating a supportive work environment, providing fair compensation, and offering growth opportunities fosters a sense of responsibility and loyalty. By investing in your employees, you build a strong foundation for exponential growth, as they become motivated, engaged, and committed to the success of the business.

Responsibility to the Community and Society:

Entrepreneurs have a unique opportunity to make a positive impact on the community and society at large. Embracing responsibility means engaging in socially responsible practices, such as environmental sustainability, ethical sourcing, and corporate philanthropy. By aligning your business with the values and needs of the community, you not only contribute to societal well-being but also enhance your brand reputation and attract customers who align with your responsible practices.

Responsibility in Business Operations:

Operating a business with responsibility requires financial prudence, legal compliance, and ethical business practices. Responsible financial management ensures stability and growth, while compliance with legal and regulatory requirements protects your business and builds trust. Ethical marketing, data privacy, and safeguarding intellectual property further demonstrate your commitment to responsible operations.

Accountability and Learning from Mistakes:

Accountability is essential for growth and improvement. Embracing responsibility means taking ownership of mistakes and failures, learning from them, and implementing corrective actions. Encouraging a growth mindset within your team fosters continuous learning and improvement. By creating a culture that embraces accountability, you pave the way for exponential growth by leveraging lessons learned from setbacks.

Key Takeaways:

1. Embrace responsibility as an entrepreneur and lead by example.

2. Prioritize exceptional customer experiences and build trust.

3. Invest in your team's well-being and professional development.

4. Engage in socially responsible practices and contribute to the community.

5. Operate with financial prudence, legal compliance, and ethical standards.

By implementing these action points, entrepreneurs can foster responsibility throughout their organizations, setting the stage for exponential business growth. Remember, responsibility is not just an obligation; it is a catalyst for success, enabling entrepreneurs to build thriving businesses that positively impact their stakeholders and the world at large. Embrace responsibility, and watch your business flourish on the path to exponential growth.

CHAPTER 5

Inside-Out Thinking: Unleashing the Power Within

Victory comes from finding opportunities in problems." – Sun Tzu

Welcome to the transformative journey of Inside-Out Thinking—an approach that empowers entrepreneurs to tap into their internal resources, values, and purpose to achieve exponential business growth. In this chapter, we will explore the concept of Inside-Out Thinking, its significance in the entrepreneurial landscape, and how it can drive remarkable success. Let us embark on a voyage of self-discovery and unleash the power within.

Understanding Inside-Out Thinking: Inside-Out Thinking is a paradigm that focuses on developing a strong internal foundation before seeking external validation. By shifting our mindset from outside influences to internal strengths, we unlock our true potential and gain a fresh perspective on business growth.

The Power of Self-Awareness:

Self-awareness is the key that unlocks the door to Inside-Out Thinking. By cultivating self-awareness, entrepreneurs gain deep insights into their values, strengths, and passions. This knowledge enables them to align personal purpose with business goals and make strategic decisions that resonate with their authentic selves.

Developing a Strong Internal Foundation: A strong internal foundation is crucial for sustainable growth. Entrepreneurs must build a positive organizational culture that fosters trust, collaboration, and open communication. By empowering and developing team members, entrepreneurs create an environment that encourages creativity and resilience—a fertile ground for exponential business growth.

Embracing Core Values and Purpose:

Core values and purpose serve as guiding stars on the journey of Inside-Out Thinking. By identifying and defining core values, entrepreneurs establish a moral compass for their business decisions. Aligning actions with these values reinforces authenticity and builds strong connections with customers. Establishing a clear and compelling purpose further ignites passion and motivates the team to pursue greatness.

Authenticity and Customer Connection:

Authenticity is the currency of Inside-Out Thinking. Entrepreneurs who embrace authenticity build genuine connections with their customers. By understanding customer needs and desires on a deeper level, entrepreneurs can create products and services that resonate. Cultivating an authentic brand and engaging in meaningful customer interactions fosters loyalty and propels exponential business growth.

Innovation and Differentiation:

Inside-Out Thinking is a catalyst for innovation and differentiation. By encouraging a culture of creativity, entrepreneurs can tap into the potential of internal resources and capabilities. Identifying unique selling propositions and competitive advantages allows entrepreneurs to stand out in a crowded marketplace. Embracing continuous improvement and adaptation ensures that the business remains relevant and stays ahead of the curve.

Overcoming Challenges and Resilience:

Challenges are an inevitable part of the entrepreneurial journey. Inside-Out Thinking equips entrepreneurs with the resilience to face setbacks and transform obstacles into opportunities. By maintaining a positive and solution-oriented mindset, entrepreneurs can leverage their internal strengths to navigate uncertainties and risks, emerging stronger and more determined.

Key Takeaways:

1. Cultivate self-awareness to align personal purpose with business goals.

2. Build a strong internal foundation through a positive organizational culture.

3. Embrace core values and purpose as guiding principles for decision-making.

4. Foster authenticity and meaningful connections with customers.

5. Encourage innovation, differentiation, and resilience to drive exponential growth.

By implementing these action points, entrepreneurs can unlock the power within themselves and their businesses. Inside-Out

Thinking empowers entrepreneurs to tap into their unique strengths, build authentic connections, and create remarkable business growth. Embrace the transformative potential of Inside-Out Thinking, and witness your entrepreneurial journey soar to new heights.

CHAPTER 6

The Power of Growth Mindset: Unleashing Exponential Business Growth

It's kind of fun to do the impossible.
- Walt Disney

Welcome to the world of growth mindset—a transformative approach that empowers entrepreneurs to achieve exponential business growth by embracing challenges, nurturing a passion for learning, and fostering resilience. In this chapter, we will explore the concept of growth mindset, its impact on entrepreneurial success, and practical strategies to cultivate it. Get ready to unlock your potential and unleash exponential business growth.

Understanding Growth Mindset: Growth mindset is a belief system that recognizes the ability to develop skills, intelligence, and talents through dedication and effort. Contrasting with a fixed mindset that believes abilities are fixed, growth mindset fuels innovation, learning, and adaptability, key ingredients for entrepreneurial success.

Embracing Challenges as Opportunities:

A growth mindset views challenges as stepping stones to growth. By reframing challenges as opportunities, entrepreneurs can embrace them with enthusiasm. They understand that setbacks and failures are valuable learning experiences that lead to improvements and innovation.

Nurturing a Passion for Learning and Development: A growth mindset thrives on continuous learning and personal development. Entrepreneurs with a growth mindset cultivate curiosity, seek new knowledge, and explore diverse perspectives. They embrace a lifelong learning journey to stay ahead in an ever-evolving business landscape.

Cultivating Resilience and Perseverance:

Resilience is the backbone of a growth mindset. Entrepreneurs with a growth mindset bounce back from setbacks, maintaining a positive attitude and an unwavering belief in their abilities. They understand that perseverance and resilience are essential for long-term success.

Embracing the Power of Effort and Persistence:

Effort and persistence are the fuel that drives exponential business growth. Entrepreneurs with a growth mindset believe that abilities can be developed through hard work, practice, and dedication. They embrace challenges, put in the necessary effort, and persist in the face of obstacles.

Fostering a Culture of Growth Mindset:

A growth mindset is contagious and can be fostered within an entrepreneurial team. Leaders play a vital role in creating a culture that values growth mindset. They model the behaviour, encourage team members to embrace challenges, provide feedback, and create an environment that celebrates learning and growth.

Overcoming Limiting Beliefs and Self-Doubt:

Limiting beliefs and self-doubt can hinder entrepreneurial success. Entrepreneurs with a growth mindset recognize and challenge these beliefs. They cultivate self-confidence, reframe negative thoughts, and focus on their strengths and potential for growth.

Leveraging the Power of Visualization and Goal Setting:

Visualization and goal setting are powerful tools for growth-minded entrepreneurs. They create a clear vision of success and set ambitious yet achievable goals. By visualizing success and breaking down goals into actionable steps, entrepreneurs can align their efforts towards exponential business growth.

Key Takeaways:

1. Embrace challenges as opportunities for growth and innovation.

2. Cultivate a passion for continuous learning and personal development.

3. Foster resilience and maintain a positive mindset in the face of setbacks.

4. Believe in the power of effort, hard work, and persistence.

5. Create a culture that nurtures and celebrates growth mindset within your entrepreneurial team.

By implementing these action points, entrepreneurs can embrace growth mindset and unlock their true potential for exponential business growth. Remember, growth mindset is not a destination but a lifelong journey. Embrace the power of growth mindset, and watch your business soar to new heights.

CHAPTER 7

Setting and Achieving Goals: The Path to Exponential Business Growth

"A goal without a timeline is just a dream."
- Robert Herjavec

Welcome to the chapter that will unlock the transformative power of goals in achieving exponential business growth. In this chapter, we will delve into the significance of goal setting, explore different types of goals, understand the SMART framework, and learn practical strategies to align, execute, and monitor goals effectively.

The Power of Setting Goals:

Setting clear and specific goals is the foundation for entrepreneurial success. Goals provide direction, focus, and motivation, acting as beacons that guide entrepreneurs towards their desired outcomes. By harnessing the power of goals, entrepreneurs can accelerate their business growth and achieve remarkable results.

Types of Goals for Business Growth:

To chart the path towards exponential growth, entrepreneurs must set different types of goals. Short-term goals drive immediate progress, long-term goals establish visionary objectives, process goals boost productivity, and outcome goals measure success and impact. By balancing these goal types, entrepreneurs can create a comprehensive roadmap for growth.

The SMART Goal-Setting Framework:

The SMART framework provides a structured approach to goal setting. Goals must be Specific, Measurable, Achievable, Relevant, and Time-bound. By applying these criteria, entrepreneurs can ensure that their goals are well-defined, trackable, realistic, aligned with their vision, and anchored within a specific timeframe.

Aligning Goals with Vision and Strategy:

Effective goal setting requires alignment with the overall vision and strategy of the business. Goals should support the overarching mission and objectives, ensuring that every milestone contributes to the long-term success of the enterprise. By aligning goals with vision and strategy, entrepreneurs create a cohesive framework for growth.

Breaking Down Goals into Actionable Steps:

To make goals achievable, entrepreneurs must break them down into actionable steps. By deconstructing long-term goals into smaller milestones, entrepreneurs create a roadmap that is easier to navigate. Developing action plans, establishing timelines, and utilizing project management tools are essential for executing goals successfully.

Monitoring Progress and Course Correction:

Monitoring goal progress is crucial to ensure success. Key Performance Indicators (KPIs) help entrepreneurs track and measure progress, providing valuable insights into the effectiveness of their strategies. Regular review and course correction allow entrepreneurs to make necessary adjustments, stay on track, and achieve their goals efficiently.

Goal Accountability and Support Systems:

Accountability plays a vital role in goal attainment. Entrepreneurs can establish accountability mechanisms, such as regular check-ins, peer reviews, or mentorship programs, to stay committed and focused. Additionally, leveraging support systems, such as mentors or accountability partners, provides encouragement and guidance throughout the goal pursuit journey.

Overcoming Obstacles and Challenges: Goal pursuit is not without its challenges. Entrepreneurs must anticipate and overcome obstacles that may arise. Strategies such as resilience, adaptability, problem-solving, and maintaining a growth mindset are crucial in navigating challenges and turning them into learning opportunities.

Key Takeaways:

1. Set clear, specific, and measurable goals aligned with your vision and strategy.

2. Break down goals into actionable steps and establish timelines for each milestone.

3. Monitor progress using key performance indicators and make necessary course corrections.

4. Foster accountability through regular check-ins and leverage support systems.

5. Embrace challenges as opportunities for growth and maintain a resilient, growth-oriented mindset.

By implementing these action points, entrepreneurs can harness the power of goal setting to drive exponential business growth. Remember, goals are not mere aspirations—they are the roadmap to success. Set your sights high, commit to your goals, and unlock the immense potential within your business.

In this chapter, we explored the significance of goal setting in achieving exponential business growth. By setting clear, SMART goals and aligning them with vision and strategy, entrepreneurs create a roadmap for success. Monitoring progress, fostering accountability, and overcoming obstacles are key elements of effective goal pursuit.

CHAPTER 8

Meeting Evolving Customer Demands: Ensuring Relevance and Business Growth

"The customer's perception is your reality."
- Kate Zabriskie

In today's fast-paced business landscape, entrepreneurs face the constant challenge of meeting evolving customer demands. This chapter explores the critical role of adapting products/ services to remain relevant and drive business growth. Through understanding customer needs, innovating offerings, enhancing customer experience, and building agile organizations, entrepreneurs can position themselves for success in an ever-changing market.

Section 1: Understanding Evolving Customer Demands

To meet evolving customer demands, it is essential to have a deep understanding of their needs and preferences. By employing various research methods, such as surveys, focus groups, and data analysis, entrepreneurs can gather valuable insights. This section highlights the significance of staying attuned to industry trends, conducting market research, and continuously seeking customer feedback to identify shifting demands.

Section 2: Adapting Existing Products/Services

Adapting existing products/services is a strategic approach to meeting evolving customer demands. By regularly assessing performance, analysing customer feedback, and monitoring market trends, entrepreneurs can identify areas for improvement. This section explores case studies and practical strategies for adapting offerings, whether through incremental enhancements or transformative updates, to stay ahead of customer expectations.

Section 3: Innovating and Introducing New Offerings

Innovation is a powerful driver of growth and relevance. This section delves into the importance of embracing innovation as a means to meet evolving customer demands. It explores different approaches, including incremental improvements, disruptive innovations, and diversification. By encouraging experimentation, prototyping, and feedback loops, entrepreneurs can continually introduce new offerings that align with emerging customer needs.

Section 4: Enhancing Customer Experience

A seamless and personalized customer experience is crucial in meeting evolving demands. This section emphasizes the connection between customer experience and business growth. It delves into the elements of a positive customer experience, such as convenience, personalization, responsiveness, and post-purchase support. Practical tips, examples, and case studies are provided to help entrepreneurs enhance customer experience and cultivate lasting customer relationships.

Section 5: Building Agile and Customer-Centric Organizations

To effectively meet evolving customer demands, entrepreneurs must build agile and customer-centric organizations. This section explores the organizational factors necessary for success. It emphasizes the importance of fostering a culture of innovation, continuous improvement, and customer-centricity. Topics such as cross-functional collaboration, agile decision-making, and employee empowerment are discussed, highlighting their significance in meeting customer demands proactively.

Meeting evolving customer demands is essential for entrepreneurs seeking exponential business growth. By adapting products/ services, embracing innovation, enhancing customer experience, and building agile organizations, entrepreneurs can stay relevant and gain a competitive edge. The chapter concludes by summarizing key takeaways and providing actionable insights for readers to implement in their businesses.

Key Takeaways:

1. Understanding customer needs and preferences is crucial for adapting products/services.
2. Regularly assess and update existing offerings to align with changing customer demands.
3. Embrace innovation and introduce new offerings to stay ahead of the competition.
4. Enhance the customer experience by focusing on convenience, personalization, and support.
5. Foster a culture of agility and customer-centricity within the organization.

Action Points:

1. Conduct regular market research and gather customer insights.

2. Analyse product/service performance and solicit customer feedback.

3. Foster a culture of innovation and experimentation within the organization.

4. Invest in technologies and processes that enhance the customer experience.

5. Encourage cross-functional collaboration and empower employees to drive customer-centric initiatives.

By incorporating these action points into their business strategies, entrepreneurs can effectively meet evolving customer demands, maintain relevance, and achieve exponential growth in a dynamic marketplace.

CHAPTER 9

Fostering a Culture of Innovation for Exponential Business Growth

"They always say time changes things, but you actually have to change them yourself."

-Steve Jobs

Imagine a workplace buzzing with excitement and creativity, where innovative ideas flow freely, and breakthrough solutions are born. This is the power of fostering a culture of innovation within your organization. In this chapter, we will delve into the significance of nurturing a culture of innovation and explore practical strategies to make it a driving force for exponential business growth.

Section 1: Understanding the Power of Innovation

Innovation is more than just a buzzword; it's the key to staying ahead in today's rapidly evolving business landscape. By constantly pushing the boundaries and seeking new ways to solve problems, businesses can achieve remarkable growth and maintain a competitive edge. Innovation fuels progress and enables organizations to adapt, evolve, and meet the changing needs of customers.

Section 2: Leadership's Role in Fostering Innovation

Leadership plays a crucial role in setting the tone for innovation within an organization. Innovative leaders inspire their teams by embracing a growth mindset and encouraging creative thinking. They foster an environment where ideas are valued, and calculated risks are encouraged. By leading by example and nurturing a culture of innovation, leaders can unleash the full potential of their employees.

Section 3: Creating an Innovation-Friendly Environment

To foster a culture of innovation, it's important to create an environment that supports and encourages it. This means breaking down hierarchical barriers and promoting open communication and idea sharing. In an innovation-friendly environment, employees feel empowered to express their ideas and collaborate with colleagues across departments. Diversity and inclusivity are also key factors that contribute to a rich tapestry of perspectives, sparking innovative thinking.

Section 4: Encouraging Creative Thinking

Creative thinking is the fuel that drives innovation. To nurture creativity, organizations can employ various techniques such as brainstorming sessions, design thinking, and ideation workshops. These approaches encourage employees to think outside the box, challenge assumptions, and explore new possibilities. By providing a safe and supportive space for creative thinking, businesses can unlock a wealth of innovative ideas.

Section 5: Promoting Collaboration and Cross-Functional Teams

Collaboration is a powerful catalyst for innovation. By fostering cross-functional teams and encouraging collaboration between different departments, organizations can tap into the diverse skills and perspectives of their employees. This interdisciplinary approach leads to fresh insights and breakthrough solutions that can revolutionize products, services, and processes. Breaking down silos and promoting a collaborative mindset is crucial to driving innovation.

Section 6: Empowering and Rewarding Innovation

Innovation thrives when employees are empowered to take ownership of their ideas and initiatives. Organizations should provide a supportive environment where employees feel encouraged to take calculated risks, experiment, and learn from failure. Recognizing and rewarding innovative efforts is also essential. Whether through financial incentives, public recognition, or career advancement opportunities, celebrating and rewarding innovation reinforces its importance and encourages a continuous cycle of innovative thinking.

Section 7: Embedding Innovation in Processes and Systems

To ensure innovation becomes ingrained in the DNA of your organization, it must be embedded in your processes and systems. Adopting agile methodologies and embracing a culture of continuous improvement allows for ongoing innovation and adaptability. By establishing feedback loops, gathering customer insights, and leveraging data-driven decision-making, businesses can continuously evolve and stay ahead of industry disruptions.

Conclusion:

Fostering a culture of innovation is not an overnight process, but it is a crucial investment for long-term business growth. By encouraging creativity, promoting collaboration, and empowering employees, organizations can unleash the full potential of their workforce and drive exponential business growth in an ever-changing world.

Key Takeaways:

1. Innovation is a powerful driver of exponential business growth and adaptability.

2. Leadership plays a pivotal role in fostering a culture of innovation within an organization.

3. Create an environment that supports and encourages

CHAPTER 10

Responding to Industry Disruptions for Exponential Business Growth

"I always tried to turn every disaster into an opportunity." - John D. Rockefeller

Imagine you're navigating through a dense forest, and suddenly you come across a new, uncharted path. You have two options: either stay stuck, hoping the old path will magically reappear, or embrace the unknown and explore the new path. In the business world, industry disruptions are like those uncharted paths. They present challenges, but they also hold immense potential for growth and success. In this chapter, we will delve into the strategies and actions you can take to respond to industry disruptions and achieve exponential business growth.

Section 1: Understanding Industry Disruptions

Industry disruptions are like earthquakes that shake the very foundations of businesses. They can be triggered by technological advancements, shifting consumer preferences, or the entry of innovative competitors. These disruptions reshape markets, challenge existing business models, and redefine customer expectations. By understanding the nature and impact of disruptions, you can proactively prepare your business for the road ahead.

Section 2: Embracing a Proactive Mindset

To respond effectively to industry disruptions, you need to develop a proactive mindset. Embrace change as an opportunity for growth rather than a threat. Be open to new ideas, trends, and technologies. Continuously scan the business environment to identify emerging trends and potential disruptions. Remember, those who resist change are left behind, while those who embrace it thrive.

Section 3: Anticipating Disruptions

The key to staying ahead of industry disruptions is anticipation. By actively monitoring the market, analysing competitors, and gathering customer feedback, you can identify early warning signs of disruptions. Stay curious and constantly seek insights that can help you anticipate and prepare for potential shifts in the industry landscape.

Section 4: Adapting Business Models

When disruptions occur, clinging to outdated business models can be detrimental. It's essential to adapt your business model to align with the changing market dynamics. Explore diversification strategies, seek strategic partnerships, and consider new distribution channels. Remember, flexibility and agility are the hallmarks of successful businesses in the face of disruption.

Section 5: Cultivating a Culture of Innovation

Innovation is the driving force behind successful responses to industry disruptions. Foster a culture of innovation within your organization. Encourage creative thinking, empower employees to experiment and take risks, and establish processes for capturing and implementing innovative ideas. Embrace a "fail fast, learn faster" mentality that encourages continuous improvement and adaptation.

Section 6: Embracing Technology and Digital Transformation

In today's digital age, technology plays a pivotal role in responding to industry disruptions. Embrace technology and leverage digital transformation to stay competitive. Explore emerging technologies such as artificial intelligence, blockchain, and automation that can streamline processes, enhance customer experiences, and create new business opportunities. Invest in digital infrastructure and equip your team with the necessary skills to leverage technology effectively.

Section 7: Collaborating with Disruptors

Rather than viewing disruptors solely as competitors, consider them as potential collaborators. Seek partnerships and collaborations with disruptors to leverage their expertise, resources, and market insights. Look for opportunities to work together, share knowledge, and create mutually beneficial relationships that can fuel growth and innovation.

Conclusion:

Industry disruptions are the new normal, and your ability to respond to them will determine the success and sustainability of your business. By embracing a proactive mindset, anticipating disruptions, adapting your business models, fostering innovation, embracing technology, and collaborating with disruptors, you can position your business for exponential growth in the face of industry disruptions.

Key Takeaways:

1. Embrace change and cultivate a proactive mindset to turn disruptions into growth opportunities.

2. Continuously monitor the market, analyze competitors, and gather customer feedback to anticipate disruptions.

3. Adapt your business models to align with changing market dynamics and customer preferences.

4. Foster a culture of innovation by encouraging creative thinking, experimentation, and continuous improvement.

5. Embrace technology and digital transformation to stay competitive and seize new business opportunities.

6. Seek partnerships and collaborations with disruptors to leverage their expertise and resources.

7. Stay agile, flexible, and ready to adapt to the ever-changing business landscape.

CHAPTER 11

Future-Proofing Your Business with Responsible Product/Services

"Strive not to be a success, but rather to be of value."- Albert Einstein

Imagine running a business that not only meets the needs of today but also anticipates and adapts to the demands of tomorrow. In this chapter, we explore the power of responsible product/services in future-proofing your business. We'll discuss how integrating sustainability, ethics, innovation, and customer-centricity can help you create a strong foundation for long-term success and make your business thrive in an ever-changing world.

Section 1: Understanding Responsible Product/ Services

Responsible product/services are more than just profit generators; they consider the larger impact on society, the environment, and ethical standards. By adopting responsible practices, you can build a reputable brand, attract conscious consumers, and mitigate risks associated with unsustainable practices. It's about creating products/services that not only benefit your bottom line but also contribute positively to the world around you.

Section 2: Identifying Future Trends and Needs

To future-proof your business, you need to be ahead of the curve. Start by understanding emerging trends, technological advancements, and evolving consumer preferences. Engage with your target audience, gather insights, and conduct market research. This knowledge will guide your product/service development, enabling you to create offerings that not only meet current demands but also anticipate future needs.

Section 3: Integrating Sustainable Practices

Sustainability is a crucial aspect of responsible product/services. Take a holistic view of your products/services and consider their environmental impact throughout their lifecycle. Explore options for using eco-friendly materials, reducing waste, and adopting renewable energy sources. By integrating sustainable practices, you not only contribute to a better world but also attract environmentally conscious consumers who value ethical businesses.

Section 4: Prioritizing Ethical Standards

Ethics should be at the core of your business. Establish a strong code of ethics that governs your product/service development process. Ensure fair labor practices, transparent supply chains, and responsible sourcing. By prioritizing ethical standards, you build trust with customers, employees, and stakeholders. This trust forms the foundation for long-term success and sets your business apart from competitors.

Section 5: Embracing Innovation and Adaptability

Innovation and adaptability are essential for future-proofing your business. Stay informed about technological advancements and industry trends. Foster a culture of innovation within your organization, where employees are encouraged to think creatively and embrace change. Explore new technologies, experiment with innovative business models, and be open to disruptive ideas that can reshape your products/services for the future.

Section 6: Customer-Centric Approach

To truly future-proof your business, you must put your customers at the center. Actively seek feedback, conduct surveys, and engage in open dialogue to understand their evolving needs. Use customer insights to refine your products/services, introduce new features, and anticipate future requirements. By staying connected with your customers, you ensure that your offerings remain relevant and your customer base remains loyal.

Future-proofing your business with responsible product/services is a proactive approach to sustainable growth. By integrating sustainability, prioritizing ethics, fostering innovation, and maintaining a customer-centric approach, you create a solid foundation for long-term success. Embrace the opportunity to make a positive impact on society and the environment while building a thriving and resilient business.

Key Takeaways:

1. Embrace responsible product/services that go beyond profit generation.

2. Stay ahead of the curve by understanding future trends and customer needs.

3. Integrate sustainable practices to reduce environmental impact and attract conscious consumers.

4. Prioritize ethical standards to build trust and maintain a positive brand reputation.

5. Foster a culture of innovation and adaptability to embrace technological advancements and market disruptions.

6. Stay customer-centric by actively seeking feedback and anticipating future requirements.

CHAPTER 12

Unleashing the Power of a Clear Value Proposition

"*Unless you have 100% customer satisfaction... you must improve.*" - Horst Schulz

Imagine walking through a bustling marketplace, surrounded by countless businesses competing for attention. In this sea of options, how can you make your business stand out? The answer lies in developing a unique selling proposition (USP) and crafting a clear value proposition that captures the essence of what makes your product or service truly special. In this chapter, we'll dive deep into the world of USPs and value propositions, exploring their importance and discovering strategies to leverage them for exponential business growth.

Section 1: Understanding the Unique Selling Proposition (USP)

Picture this: You stumble upon a digital marketing agency called "Digital Dynamo." Intrigued, you strike up a conversation with the owner, Sarah. As she shares her story, you learn that her business experienced rapid growth in its early years. However, as the market evolved, her growth started to stagnate. Sarah realized that she needed a compelling USP to differentiate herself and rekindle her business's growth.

Sarah's journey is a testament to the power of a USP. It's what sets your business apart from the competition and grabs the attention of your target audience. By identifying your differentiating factors and understanding your audience's needs, desires, and pain points, you can develop a USP that resonates and compels customers to choose you.

Section 2: Crafting a Compelling Value Proposition

Now that you grasp the importance of a USP, let's explore how to craft a compelling value proposition. Imagine Sarah sitting down with her team at Digital Dynamo, brainstorming ways to clearly articulate the value they provide to customers. They realize that it's not enough to list the features of their services; they must emphasize the benefits customers will experience by choosing them.

Your value proposition should answer the fundamental question of "Why should customers choose us?" It should communicate the unique value you bring to the table and how it solves your customers' problems or fulfills their needs. Remember to strike a balance between emotional and rational appeal, appealing to customers' hearts while showcasing the practical benefits they'll enjoy.

Section 3: Communicating Your Value Proposition

Crafting a compelling value proposition is just the first step. To make an impact, you must effectively communicate it to your target audience. Imagine Sarah revamping Digital Dynamo's website, ensuring that their value proposition shines through every page. They create a concise and memorable elevator pitch that captures their unique value in a way that sticks with potential clients.

Consistency is key when communicating your value proposition. It should be seamlessly integrated across all marketing channels, from your website to social media and advertising campaigns. Think visually and verbally, using captivating design elements and clear, compelling copy to reinforce your value proposition and leave a lasting impression.

Section 4: Leveraging Your Value Proposition for Business Growth.

Now that you have a compelling value proposition, it's time to leverage it for business growth. Sarah and her team at Digital Dynamo understand the importance of targeted marketing and positioning. By aligning their value proposition with their target market and highlighting their unique advantages, they attract the right customers and differentiate themselves from competitors.

Building trust and loyalty is crucial. Sarah knows that to foster long-term relationships, they must consistently deliver on their promises and communicate their value proposition authentically. By building trust, they secure customer loyalty and create brand advocates who help fuel their business growth.

Section 5: Evolving Your Value Proposition

The market is constantly evolving, and customer needs change with time. Sarah and her team at Digital Dynamo understand that to remain relevant, they must continuously refine and adapt their value proposition. They actively seek customer feedback, conduct market research, and stay informed about emerging trends and technologies.

Innovation plays a vital role in future-proofing your value proposition. Sarah encourages her team to think outside the box, embracing new ideas and approaches. By leveraging innovation and adapting to changing customer preferences, they stay ahead of the curve and ensure their value proposition remains compelling.

Crafting a clear value proposition backed by a strong USP is a powerful tool for business growth. By understanding your differentiating factors, defining your value proposition, effectively communicating it, and leveraging it to differentiate yourself and build trust, you can propel your business to new heights of success.

Key Takeaways:

1. Define your unique selling proposition (USP) by identifying what sets you apart from competitors.

2. Craft a compelling value proposition that clearly communicates the unique value you offer to customers.

3. Focus on the benefits customers will experience, rather than just listing product features.

4. Consistently communicate your value proposition across all marketing channels.

5. Leverage your value proposition to refine your target market, differentiate yourself from competitors, and build trust and loyalty.

6. Continuously refine and adapt your value proposition to meet changing customer needs and market trends.

Action Points:

1. Conduct a thorough analysis of your business and identify your unique strengths, expertise, and differentiating factors.

2. Develop a clear and concise value proposition that focuses on the benefits customers will gain from choosing your product or service.

3. Ensure your value proposition is consistently communicated across all marketing channels, including your website, social media, and advertising campaigns.

4. Gather customer feedback and conduct market research to refine and enhance your value proposition based on evolving customer needs.

5. Embrace innovation and stay ahead of the curve by actively seeking new ideas and approaches to continuously improve and adapt your value proposition.

CHAPTER 13

Being a Differentiator

"Change the way you look at things and the things you look at change." - Wayne W. Dyer

Imagine being in a crowded marketplace where countless businesses are vying for the attention of customers. How can you ensure that your business stands out and captures the hearts of your target audience? In this chapter, we will explore the art of being a differentiator from competitors and discuss strategies to help you carve your unique path to exponential business growth.

Section 1: Understanding Your Competitive Landscape To become a strong differentiator, start by understanding your competitive landscape. Take a closer look at your industry or niche. Identify key competitors and study their strengths and weaknesses. By assessing the market trends and dynamics that impact competition, you can gain valuable insights into where you fit in and how you can stand out.

Section 2: Defining Your Unique Value Proposition A crucial step in differentiating yourself is defining your Unique Value Proposition (UVP). What makes your business special? Identify your core strengths, unique offerings, and competitive advantages. Craft a compelling UVP that clearly communicates the value you provide to customers. Your UVP should resonate with your target audience and highlight the benefits they can expect by choosing your business.

Section 3: Emphasizing Your Brand Identity Your brand identity plays a significant role in setting you apart from competitors. Develop a strong and authentic brand identity that speaks to your target audience. Create a unique brand story that captures the essence of your business and showcases your values. Consistently communicate your brand message across all touchpoints to reinforce your differentiation and build a memorable brand presence.

Section 4: Delivering Exceptional Customer Experience One of the most effective ways to differentiate yourself is by delivering exceptional customer experiences. Take the time to understand your customers' needs and expectations. Design customer-centric processes and experiences that go above and beyond. Personalize interactions, exceed expectations, and build strong relationships with your customers. By providing outstanding service, you'll stand out from competitors who may neglect the customer experience.

Section 5: Innovating and Staying Ahead To remain a differentiator, embrace a culture of innovation and continuous improvement. Anticipate market trends and customer demands to stay ahead of the competition. Be proactive in developing new products, services, or features that address evolving customer needs. By constantly innovating, you can ensure that you're always offering something unique and valuable to your target audience.

Section 6: Marketing and Positioning Strategies Your marketing and positioning strategies are essential tools for differentiation. Develop a targeted marketing strategy that highlights your unique selling points. Showcase your UVP, brand identity, and exceptional customer experiences through various marketing channels. Leverage digital marketing and social media platforms to amplify your message and engage with your audience effectively.

Section 7: Building Strategic Partnerships Strategic partnerships can help you differentiate your business and expand your reach. Explore collaborations with like-minded businesses that complement your offerings. Identify synergistic alliances that enable you to access new markets or customer segments. By leveraging the expertise and resources of strategic partners, you can enhance your competitive advantage and create unique opportunities for growth.

Being a differentiator from competitors is a key driver of exponential business growth. By understanding your competitive landscape, defining a compelling Unique Value Proposition, emphasizing your brand identity, delivering exceptional customer experiences, fostering innovation, implementing effective marketing strategies, and building strategic partnerships, you can successfully differentiate yourself and create a lasting impact in the market.

Key Takeaways:

1. Research your competitive landscape to gain insights into your industry and competitors.

2. Define a compelling Unique Value Proposition that clearly communicates your business's value.

3. Develop a strong and authentic brand identity that resonates with your target audience.

4. Focus on delivering exceptional customer experiences to build loyalty and stand out from competitors.

5. Embrace innovation, anticipate market trends, and constantly offer new

CHAPTER 14

Targeted Marketing: Hitting the Bullseye for Exponential Growth

"Marketing is no longer about the stuff you make but about the stories you tell." - Seth Godin

In today's fast-paced and competitive business landscape, reaching the right audience is crucial for success. Targeted marketing is the art of identifying and engaging with your ideal customers, allowing you to maximize your resources, increase conversion rates, and achieve exponential business growth. In this chapter, we will explore the power of targeted marketing and how you can leverage it to propel your business forward.

Section 1: Understanding Your Ideal Customer The foundation of targeted marketing is understanding your ideal customer. Dive deep into your customer data and market research to create detailed buyer personas. Identify their demographics, interests, pain points, and buying behaviours. By knowing who your audience is, you can tailor your marketing efforts to resonate with them effectively.

Section 2: Tailoring Your Message Crafting a message that speaks directly to your target audience is essential. Develop personalized and relevant content that addresses the specific needs and preferences of your ideal customers. Tailor you're messaging across various marketing channels to create a consistent and impactful brand experience.

Section 3: Utilizing Data and Analytics Data and analytics play a critical role in targeted marketing. Leverage tools and technologies to gather valuable insights about your customers' behaviours and interactions with your brand. Analyze the data to make informed decisions and optimize your marketing strategies. Data-driven marketing allows you to refine your approach and ensure you are always hitting the bullseye with your campaigns.

Section 4: Choosing the Right Marketing Channels Not all marketing channels are created equal. Select the ones that align with your target audience's preferences and behaviours. Whether it's social media, email marketing, content marketing, SEO, or paid advertising, understanding where your customers are and how they engage with brands will guide you in choosing the most effective channels.

Section 5: Implementing Personalization goes beyond addressing your customers by their names. Implement dynamic content and product recommendations based on their past interactions and preferences. By tailoring the customer journey, you create a more meaningful and engaging experience, increasing the likelihood of conversion and brand loyalty.

Section 6: A/B Testing and Optimization Continuous improvement is key in targeted marketing. Implement A/B testing to compare different marketing elements and identify what resonates best with your audience. Use the insights gained from testing to optimize your campaigns and strategies for better results.

Section 7: Leveraging social media Targeting Social media platforms offer robust targeting capabilities that allow you to reach specific demographics, interests, and behaviours. Develop targeted social media campaigns to connect with your ideal customers and build a community around your brand.

Section 8: Partnering with Influencers Influencers can be powerful advocates for your brand, especially when their audience aligns with your target market. Collaborate with influencers who share your values and have a genuine connection with your ideal customers. Their endorsements can significantly impact brand awareness and credibility.

Conclusion: Targeted marketing is a potent tool for entrepreneurs seeking exponential business growth. By understanding your ideal customer, tailoring your messaging, leveraging data and analytics, choosing the right marketing channels, implementing personalization, conducting A/B testing, leveraging social media targeting, and partnering with influencers, you can elevate your marketing efforts to new heights and achieve remarkable results.

Key Takeaways:

1. Understand your ideal customer through detailed buyer personas and market research.
2. Craft personalized and relevant messaging that resonates with your target audience.
3. Leverage data and analytics to make informed marketing decisions and optimizations.
4. Choose the most effective marketing channels that align with your target audience's preferences.
5. Implement personalization and continuous A/B testing to refine your marketing strategies.

CHAPTER 15

Enhancing Your Brand Image: Unleashing the Power of Perception

"Design is the silent ambassador of your brand."
- Paul Rand

Let's explore the fascinating world of brand image and learn how to enhance and optimize the perception of your business. In this highly competitive marketplace, a strong brand image can be a game-changer, setting you apart from competitors and driving exponential business growth. So, let's dive in and discover the secrets to crafting an enhanced brand image that captivates your audience.

Section 1: Defining Brand Image

Before we dive into strategies for enhancing your brand image, let's start by understanding what brand image is all about. Brand image encompasses the emotions, beliefs, and associations that customers have with your brand. It goes beyond just a logo or a tagline – it's the overall perception people have when they think of your business. A positive brand image can build customer loyalty, trust, and create a lasting impact on your bottom line.

Section 2: Crafting Your Brand Story

One of the most powerful ways to enhance your brand image is by crafting a compelling brand story. Your brand story should encapsulate your core values, mission, and vision in a way that resonates deeply with your target audience. It's about connecting with them on an emotional level, sharing your journey, and highlighting what sets you apart from competitors. A captivating brand story creates a strong foundation for your brand image.

Section 3: Consistent Branding and Visual Identity

Consistency is key when it comes to building a strong brand image. Your visual identity, including your logo, colours, typography, and overall design, should be consistent across all touchpoints. Whether it's your website, packaging, social media profiles, or marketing materials, maintaining a cohesive visual identity creates a sense of professionalism and reinforces brand recognition.

Section 4: Building Trust and Credibility

Trust and credibility are crucial elements of a strong brand image. To enhance these qualities, you must deliver on your promises, provide exceptional customer service, and maintain transparent communication with your audience. When customers trust your brand, they are more likely to become loyal advocates and recommend your business to others. Demonstrating your expertise and thought leadership through content marketing, speaking engagements, and industry collaborations also boosts credibility.

Section 5: Engaging and Building a Community

Your brand image is not just about what you say, but how you engage with your audience. Actively engaging and building a community around your brand helps foster meaningful connections and strengthens your brand image. Utilize social media platforms to interact with your audience, respond to their comments and inquiries, and show appreciation for their support. Encourage user-generated content and customer testimonials to showcase positive experiences and build social proof.

Section 6: Influencer and Partnership Marketing

Leveraging the power of influencers and strategic partnerships can significantly enhance your brand image. Collaborating with influencers who align with your brand values and have a strong following allows you to tap into their audience and build credibility through association. Additionally, seek partnerships with complementary brands or organizations to reach new audiences and create mutually beneficial campaigns that elevate your brand image.

Section 7: Corporate Social Responsibility and Purpose-Driven Initiatives

In today's socially conscious world, embracing corporate social responsibility (CSR) and purpose-driven initiatives is not only good for the planet but also for your brand image. Align your brand with social causes and take meaningful actions to make a positive impact. Share stories of how your business is contributing to a better world, whether it's through sustainability efforts, philanthropy, or community involvement. Authenticity and genuine commitment to CSR can enhance your brand image and resonate with socially conscious consumers.

Congratulations! You've gained valuable insights into enhancing your brand image and unleashing the power of perception. By crafting a compelling brand story, maintaining consistent branding, building trust and credibility, engaging with your audience, leveraging influencers and partnerships, and embracing corporate social responsibility, you can elevate your brand image and position your business for exponential growth.

Key Takeaways:

1. Craft a compelling brand story that connects emotionally with your target audience.

2. Maintain a consistent visual identity across all touchpoints to reinforce brand recognition.

3. Deliver on promises, provide exceptional customer service, and communicate transparently to build trust and credibility.

4. Actively engage with your audience, foster meaningful connections, and build a community around your brand.

5. Leverage influencers and strategic partnerships, and embrace corporate social responsibility to enhance your brand image and reach.

Remember, enhancing your brand image is an ongoing journey. Continually evaluate and refine your strategies to ensure that your brand image aligns with your business goals and resonates with your target audience. Good luck on your brand-building adventure!

CHAPTER 16

Attracting and Retaining Top Talent: Building a Dream Team for Exponential Business Growth

"Talent wins games, but teamwork and intelligence win championships." – Michael Jordan

Let us dive into the exciting world of attracting and retaining top talent. Your team is the lifeblood of your business, and having the right people on board can make all the difference in achieving exponential growth. We'll explore strategies to attract top talent, create a positive work environment, and implement effective retention strategies. By the end of this chapter, you'll be equipped with actionable insights to build a dream team that drives your business to new heights.

Section 1: Defining Your Ideal Team

To attract the right talent, it's essential to define your ideal team. Take some time to identify the skills, experiences, and qualities that are crucial for your business. Consider the roles and responsibilities you need to fill and the specific talents that will help your business thrive. Having this clarity will guide your recruitment efforts and ensure you find candidates who align with your goals and values.

Section 2: Crafting a Compelling Employer Brand

Building a strong employer brand is a powerful tool for attracting top talent. Think of your employer brand as your business's reputation as an employer. Define your company culture, values, and unique selling points that set you apart. Showcase your brand through your website, social media, and other marketing channels. Use employee testimonials and success stories to reinforce the appeal of working for your organization.

Section 3: Effective Recruitment Strategies

Now that you have a clear vision of your ideal team and a compelling employer brand, it's time to implement effective recruitment strategies. Start by creating comprehensive job descriptions that clearly outline expectations and responsibilities. Then, leverage various channels such as job boards, social media platforms, and professional networks to reach a diverse pool of candidates. Don't forget the power of employee referrals—your existing team members can be a valuable source for finding top talent.

Section 4: Creating a Positive Work Environment

Once you've attracted talented individuals, it's crucial to create a positive work environment that keeps them engaged and motivated. Foster a culture of collaboration, open communication, and continuous learning. Provide opportunities for professional growth and development, such as training programs, mentorship, and skill-building initiatives. Ensure that your workplace is supportive and inclusive, valuing diversity and encouraging innovation.

Section 5: Competitive Compensation and Benefits

Offering competitive compensation and benefits is essential for attracting and retaining top talent. Research industry standards and ensure that your salary and benefits packages are in line with market expectations. Consider additional perks and incentives that differentiate you from competitors, such as flexible working hours, remote work options, wellness programs, and performance-based bonuses. Find ways to show your team members that their contributions are valued and rewarded.

Section 6: Employee Engagement and Recognition

Engaging your employees and recognizing their contributions is crucial for creating a positive work culture. Foster open lines of communication, actively listen to their feedback, and involve them in decision-making processes whenever possible. Implement recognition programs to celebrate achievements and milestones. Regularly provide feedback and opportunities for growth to keep your team members motivated and committed to your business.

Section 7: Professional Development and Growth Opportunities

Investing in your employees' professional development is a win-win situation. Offer opportunities for skill-building, training, and attending conferences or industry events. Create a career path within your organization, providing clear advancement opportunities and promoting from within whenever possible. Regularly assess individual goals and aspirations, aligning them with your company's growth plans. By investing in their growth, you create a sense of loyalty and commitment among your team members.

Section 8: Work-Life Balance and Well-being

Supporting work-life balance and prioritizing employee well-being is crucial for retention. Offer flexible work arrangements to accommodate personal needs and commitments. Promote a healthy work-life balance by encouraging employees to take breaks, vacations, and recharge. Provide resources for mental and physical well-being, such as wellness programs, employee assistance programs, and access to healthcare benefits. Show genuine care for your team's overall well-being, and they will be more motivated and dedicated to your business.

Key Takeaways:

1. Define your ideal team and the skills necessary for success.
2. Craft a compelling employer brand to attract top talent.
3. Implement effective recruitment strategies to reach a diverse pool of candidates.
4. Create a positive work environment that fosters collaboration, growth, and innovation.
5. Offer competitive compensation, benefits, and opportunities for professional development to retain your top performers.

Action Points:

1. Conduct a thorough assessment of your ideal team requirements and align them with your business goals.

2. Develop a comprehensive employer brand strategy that highlights your unique selling points.

3. Review and enhance your recruitment strategies to attract top talent from various channels.

4. Evaluate your current work environment and implement changes to create a positive and inclusive culture.

5. Conduct a compensation and benefits analysis to ensure your offerings are competitive and attractive to top performers.

Remember, building a dream team takes time and effort, but the rewards are immeasurable. By attracting and retaining top talent, you create a solid foundation for exponential business growth. Good luck on your journey to building an exceptional team!

CHAPTER 17

Building a Strong Organizational Culture: Unleashing the Power of Values and Beliefs

"Culture eats strategy for breakfast."

- Peter Drucker

The importance of building a strong organizational culture and how it can fuel your business's growth and success cannot be undermined. Think of your organizational culture as the DNA of your company—a set of shared values, beliefs, and behaviours that guide your team's actions and shape your work environment. In this chapter, we'll delve into the key components of organizational culture, understand its impact on employee engagement and performance, and learn strategies for building and nurturing a positive and impactful culture that drives exponential business growth.

Section 1: Understanding Organizational Culture

Organizational culture is the invisible force that permeates your company and influences how your team members think, behave, and interact. It consists of shared values, beliefs, and assumptions that serve as the foundation for decision-making and actions. Understanding these components and their impact on your business is crucial for shaping a strong culture aligned with your goals and values. We'll also explore the role of leadership in shaping and fostering the desired culture.

Section 2: The Impact of Organizational Culture

A strong organizational culture has a profound impact on your business. It shapes employee behaviour, engagement, and performance. When your culture is positive and aligned with your values, it promotes teamwork, collaboration, and innovation. It also plays a crucial role in attracting and retaining top talent and creating a positive customer experience. We'll delve into these dynamics and discover how a strong culture contributes to your business's growth and success.

Section 3: Building a Positive Organizational Culture

Building a positive organizational culture requires a deliberate and proactive approach. We'll explore practical strategies for defining and communicating your desired culture, ensuring it aligns with your business goals and values. Creating a culture of open communication, trust, and transparency is essential for fostering an environment where everyone feels valued and engaged. We'll also delve into the role of rituals, traditions, and celebrations in reinforcing your culture and creating a sense of belonging.

Section 4: Nurturing and Sustaining Your Organizational Culture

Building a strong culture is an ongoing process that requires consistent effort and attention. We'll discuss the importance of consistent leadership behaviors in shaping and reinforcing your culture. Ongoing feedback and learning play a crucial role in nurturing your culture and driving continuous improvement. We'll also address how to navigate organizational change while preserving your culture, as well as the role of performance management in aligning behaviors with your desired culture.

Section5:MeasuringandAssessingYourOrganizational Culture

Measuring and assessing your organizational culture is essential for understanding its effectiveness and identifying areas for improvement. We'll explore different methods and tools for measuring culture, such as employee surveys, focus groups, and cultural assessments. We'll discuss how to interpret the results and take actionable steps to enhance your culture where needed. Regularly assessing your culture ensures that it remains aligned with your evolving business needs.

Key Takeaways:

1. Organizational culture is the collective values, beliefs, and behaviours that shape your work environment and influence employee behaviour and performance.

2. A strong and positive culture fosters teamwork, collaboration, innovation, and enhances employee engagement.

3. Building a positive culture requires defining and communicating your desired culture, fostering open communication, and aligning behaviours with your values.

4. Nurturing and sustaining your culture involves consistent leadership, ongoing feedback, embracing change while preserving core values, and creating rituals and traditions that reinforce your culture.

5. Measuring and assessing your culture helps identify areas for improvement and take proactive steps to enhance it over time.

Action Points:

1. Define your desired organizational culture, ensuring alignment with your business values and goals.

2. Communicate and reinforce your culture through consistent messaging and visible leadership behaviours.

3. Foster open communication and create opportunities for feedback and dialogue within your organization.

4. Celebrate and recognize behaviours that align with your culture to reinforce desired behaviours.

5. Regularly assess and measure your culture to identify areas for improvement and take appropriate action.

By consciously cultivating a strong organizational culture, you create an environment that empowers your team, fosters innovation, and drives exponential business growth. Embrace the power of values and beliefs, and watch your organization thrive.

CHAPTER 18

Enhancing Productivity: Unleashing the Potential for Exponential Business Growth

"Productivity is being able to do things that you were never able to do before."- Franz Kafka

Get ready to unlock the hidden potential within your business and propel it towards exponential growth through enhanced productivity. In this chapter, we'll explore powerful strategies and techniques that will revolutionize the way you and your team work. By implementing these practices, you'll witness a remarkable surge in productivity, pushing your business to new heights.

Section 1: Understanding Productivity

Productivity is the cornerstone of success. It's about accomplishing more in less time, harnessing your resources effectively, and achieving outstanding results. We'll delve into the true meaning of productivity and its multi-dimensional nature. By understanding its intricacies, you'll be equipped with the knowledge needed to transform your work approach.

Section 2: Creating a Productive Work Environment

Imagine stepping into an environment that fuels your motivation, ignites your creativity, and propels you to surpass your limits. We'll explore the power of a productive work environment and how it can be a catalyst for success. From optimizing your workspace to embracing technology, you'll learn how to create a dynamic and inspiring atmosphere that propels productivity to unprecedented levels.

Section 3: Effective Time Management

Time is a precious commodity that, when managed wisely, can work wonders. We'll unlock the secrets of effective time management, allowing you to seize every moment and make the most of it. Discover the art of setting goals, prioritizing tasks, and maximizing your daily output. Embrace the power of delegation and outsourcing, freeing up valuable time for more important endeavours.

Section 4: Streamlining Workflows and Processes

Inefficiency can be a silent productivity killer. It's time to banish it once and for all. We'll delve into the world of streamlined workflows and optimized processes, where every action contributes to your business's success. Learn the art of process mapping, embrace automation, and unleash the power of continuous improvement. By doing so, you'll eliminate bottlenecks and propel your productivity to new heights.

Section 5: Empowering and Engaging Your Team

A team is only as strong as its members. We'll explore the magic of empowerment and engagement, which are essential for enhancing productivity. Learn to inspire and lead your team towards greatness. Foster a culture of accountability, provide growth opportunities, and encourage work-life balance. By doing so, you'll ignite a spark within your team, leading to exceptional results.

Key Takeaways:

1. Productivity is the key to unlocking exponential growth and achieving outstanding results.

2. Creating a productive work environment fuels motivation and creativity.

3. Effective time management empowers you to make the most of each moment.

4. Streamlining workflows and processes eliminates inefficiencies and boosts productivity.

5. Empowering and engaging your team unleashes their potential and drives remarkable results.

Action Points:

1. Assess your current productivity levels and identify areas for improvement.

2. Implement time management techniques such as goal setting, task prioritization, and delegation.

3. Streamline workflows and processes through process mapping, automation, and continuous improvement initiatives.

4. Foster a productive work environment by optimizing your workspace, embracing technology, and promoting creativity.

5. Empower and engage your team through effective leadership, accountability, growth opportunities, and work-life balance initiatives.

By embracing enhanced productivity, you'll revolutionize the way you work and propel your business towards exponential growth. Remember, you have the power to achieve greatness. Embrace these strategies, ignite your team's potential, and watch your business soar to new heights. Get ready to unleash your productivity and seize the success you deserve!

CHAPTER 19

Operational Efficiency

"If you define the problem correctly, you almost have the solution." - Steve Jobs

Get ready to supercharge your business operations and unlock its full potential for exponential growth. In this chapter, we'll dive deep into the world of operational efficiency and explore strategies that will revolutionize the way you run your business. By optimizing your operations, you'll not only increase profitability but also enhance customer satisfaction and drive your business towards unparalleled success. So, let's ignite the spark of efficiency and propel your business to new heights!

Section 1: Understanding Operational Efficiency

Operational efficiency is the secret sauce that sets successful businesses apart. It's the foundation upon which growth and profitability are built. Picture a well-oiled machine, where every part works seamlessly together, eliminating waste and maximizing output. By understanding the importance of efficiency, you'll be motivated to harness its power to transform your business.

Section 2: Process Analysis and Improvement

To unlock the true potential of your business, it's crucial to analyze and improve your processes. Imagine dissecting each step, identifying inefficiencies, and eliminating obstacles that hinder productivity. Through process mapping and careful examination, you'll uncover hidden opportunities for improvement. Embrace the mindset of continuous improvement and challenge the status quo to create a leaner, more efficient operation.

Section 3: Leveraging Technology and Automation

In the digital age, technology offers a plethora of tools to optimize your operations. Embrace automation, artificial intelligence, and software solutions that can streamline your processes, save time, and enhance accuracy. Picture the repetitive tasks being handled effortlessly, freeing up your team to focus on value-added activities. Embrace technology as a powerful ally in your pursuit of operational excellence.

Section 4: Data-Driven Decision Making

Data is the compass that guides you towards efficiency. Embrace the power of data-driven decision making. Collect and analyse relevant metrics to gain valuable insights into your operations. Uncover patterns, identify trends, and make informed decisions that propel your business forward. Let data be your trusted advisor, leading you to smarter, more efficient choices.

Section 5: Continuous Improvement and Agile Practices

Optimizing operational efficiency is not a one-time effort, but a continuous journey. Embrace the concept of continuous improvement and agile practices. Encourage a culture of experimentation, innovation, and adaptation. Empower your team to share their insights, ideas, and suggestions for process enhancements. Foster an environment where everyone is committed to finding better, more efficient ways of doing things.

Key Takeaways:

1. Operational efficiency is the key to unlocking exponential business growth and profitability.
2. Process analysis and improvement are crucial for identifying and eliminating inefficiencies.
3. Technology and automation can streamline operations, save time, and enhance accuracy.
4. Data-driven decision making empowers you to make informed choices that drive efficiency.
5. Embrace a culture of continuous improvement and agility to stay ahead of the competition.

Action Points:

1. Conduct a thorough process analysis to identify inefficiencies and bottlenecks.
2. Embrace technology solutions that automate manual tasks and streamline operations.
3. Establish a data-driven approach, collecting and analyzing key metrics to drive efficiency.
4. Foster a culture of continuous improvement, encouraging employees to share process enhancement ideas.
5. Embrace agility, allowing for flexibility and adaptation in a dynamic business environment.

Remember, optimizing operational efficiency is a journey, not a destination. Stay motivated, stay committed, and embrace the power of efficiency. Streamline your processes, leverage technology, make data-driven decisions, and foster a culture of continuous improvement. Your business is ready to soar to new heights of success and profitability. Take action today and unleash the power of operational efficiency!

CHAPTER 20

Driving Customer Engagement: Igniting the Passion of Your Audience

"If you are not taking care of your customers, your competitor will." - Bob Hooey

Get ready to unlock the power of customer engagement and ignite the passion of your audience. In this chapter, we'll delve into the strategies and tactics that will help you build strong connections, foster loyalty, and create a thriving community of brand enthusiasts. Customer engagement is the fuel that propels your business forward, and by mastering it, you'll experience exponential growth. So, let's dive in and discover the secrets to driving customer engagement with passion and purpose!

Section 1: The Power of Customer Engagement

Every interaction with your customers is an opportunity to create a lasting impression. Customer engagement goes beyond mere transactions; it's about building emotional connections. Engaged customers are not just buyers; they are advocates who are passionate about your brand. When you harness the power of customer engagement, you'll experience increased customer loyalty, enthusiastic word-of-mouth referrals, and a strong brand presence that sets you apart from the competition.

Section 2: Understanding Your Customers

To drive customer engagement, you must deeply understand your target audience. Take the time to dive into their world, uncover their needs, desires, and pain points. Develop detailed buyer personas that capture their motivations, preferences, and behaviours. Armed with this knowledge, you can tailor your engagement strategies to resonate with your customers on a personal level. Remember, empathy is the key to forging genuine connections.

Section 3: Crafting Compelling Content

Content is the heartbeat of customer engagement. Create compelling content that captivates your audience, educates them, and adds value to their lives. Whether it's through captivating blog posts, informative videos, or engaging social media campaigns, your content should speak directly to the hearts and minds of your customers. Craft a content strategy that aligns with their interests and aspirations, and watch as they become actively engaged in your brand's story.

Section 4: Building a Community

Customers crave a sense of belonging and connection. By building a vibrant community around your brand, you create an ecosystem where customers can interact with each other, share their experiences, and feel like they are part of something greater. Create online and offline platforms where customers can engage, ask questions, provide feedback, and find support. Foster a community that amplifies your brand's reach and influence, and watch as your engaged customers become your brand advocates.

Section 5: Embracing Personalization and Omnichannel Engagement

In today's digital landscape, customers expect personalized experiences that cater to their unique preferences and needs. Leverage data and technology to deliver personalized recommendations, targeted offers, and customized communications. Embrace omnichannel engagement, ensuring a consistent and seamless experience across various touchpoints, from social media to email marketing and beyond. By providing a personalized and connected journey, you'll deepen customer engagement and loyalty.

Key Takeaways:

1. Customer engagement is about building emotional connections and meaningful relationships.
2. Deeply understand your target audience to tailor your engagement strategies effectively.
3. Compelling content adds value and captivates your audience's attention.
4. Foster a vibrant community where customers can connect, share, and advocate for your brand.
5. Embrace personalization and provide a seamless omnichannel experience to enhance engagement.

Action Points:

1. Conduct thorough market research to develop detailed buyer personas and gain deep insights into your target audience.

2. Create a content strategy that aligns with your customers' interests, aspirations, and pain points, offering valuable insights and solutions.

3. Build an online community platform where customers can connect, interact, and share their experiences.

4. Leverage data and technology to personalize customer experiences, delivering tailored recommendations and communications.

5. Embrace an omnichannel approach, ensuring a seamless and consistent customer journey across

CHAPTER 21

Enhanced Customer Insights: Unveiling the Secrets to Understanding Your Customers

"*Customer service should not be a department. It should be the entire company.*" - Tony Hsieh

Get ready to unlock the hidden secrets of enhanced customer insights and revolutionize your business growth. Imagine having a deep understanding of your customers, knowing their desires, preferences, and motivations. By harnessing the power of enhanced customer insights, you can create personalized experiences, make informed decisions, and build lasting relationships with your audience. In this chapter, we will dive into the significance of customer insights and explore practical strategies to gather, analyse, and leverage data. Let's embark on this exciting journey of uncovering valuable customer insights!

Section 1: The Significance of Customer Insights

Customer insights are the key to unlocking the hearts and minds of your customers. They go beyond surface-level knowledge and allow you to truly understand what makes your customers tick. By gathering and analysing relevant data, you gain a competitive edge and can tailor your offerings to meet their needs and desires. Enhanced customer insights empower you to make data-driven decisions, design targeted marketing campaigns, and create exceptional customer experiences.

Section 2: Collecting Customer Data

To gain valuable customer insights, you need to collect data from various sources. This includes both quantitative and qualitative data. Dive deep into demographics, purchase history, website analytics, and social media interactions. Implement robust data collection methods and leverage technology to capture accurate and comprehensive information about your customers. Remember, data is the fuel that powers your understanding of customers.

Section 3: Analysing Customer Data

Collecting data is just the beginning; the real magic lies in analysing and interpreting that data. Utilize data analytics techniques to uncover patterns, trends, and correlations within your customer data. Seek actionable insights that can drive your business growth. Embrace the power of advanced analytics tools and algorithms to extract valuable nuggets of information from your data goldmine.

Section 4: Creating Customer Personas

Customer personas bring your data to life. They are detailed representations of your ideal customers, based on real data and insights. Develop vivid customer personas that capture the essence of your target audience. Go beyond demographics and explore their behaviours, preferences, goals, and pain points. Customer personas serve as guiding stars, helping you align your marketing efforts and deliver personalized experiences that resonate with your customers.

Section 5: Implementing Customer Feedback Mechanisms

Your customers hold valuable insights. Implement mechanisms such as surveys, reviews, and feedback forms to actively gather their opinions. Encourage open and honest communication, and leverage the feedback to continuously improve your products, services, and customer experiences. Embrace the power of customer feedback as a compass guiding you towards customer-centric excellence.

Section 6: Leveraging Technology for Customer Insights

Technology is a catalyst for enhanced customer insights. Implement customer relationship management (CRM) systems, data analytics tools, and artificial intelligence (AI) solutions to streamline data collection, analysis, and interpretation. Leverage the power of automation and advanced technologies to identify patterns, uncover hidden insights, and deliver exceptional customer experiences.

Key Takeaways:

1. Enhanced customer insights unlock a deep understanding of your customers' needs, preferences, and motivations.

2. Collect diverse data sources, both quantitative and qualitative, to paint a comprehensive picture of your customers.

3. Analyse customer data using advanced analytics techniques to extract actionable insights for informed decision-making.

4. Develop detailed customer personas that capture the essence of your target audience and guide your marketing efforts.

5. Implement customer feedback mechanisms and leverage technology to gather feedback, improve experiences, and drive growth.

Action Points:

1. Define the key data points relevant to your business and establish effective data collection strategies.

2. Invest in data analytics tools and resources to analyse customer data and uncover valuable insights.

3. Create detailed customer personas based on the collected insights and align your marketing efforts accordingly.

4. Implement customer feedback mechanisms, such as surveys or review platforms, to gather valuable feedback and make improvements.

5. Embrace technology solutions, such as CRM systems and AI tools, to streamline data management and leverage advanced analytics capabilities.

You now understand the significance of enhanced customer insights and how they can fuel your business growth. By collecting, analyzing, and leveraging customer data, you can uncover valuable insights that drive personalized experiences, informed decision-making, and stronger customer relationships. Remember, customer insights are a continuous journey. Stay curious, adapt to evolving customer needs, and use technology to your advantage. Let the power of enhanced customer insights propel your business to new heights!

CHAPTER 22

Unlocking Growth: Upselling and Cross-selling Opportunities

"Wish it. Plan it. Do it." - Jaipal Singh

Prepare to embark on a journey of growth and profitability as we explore the remarkable world of upselling and cross-selling opportunities. These strategies hold the key to unlocking exponential business growth by tapping into the untapped potential within your existing customer base. Get ready to supercharge your revenue, delight your customers, and propel your business to new heights.

Section 1: The Power of Upselling and Cross-selling

In today's fiercely competitive market, simply acquiring new customers is no longer enough. The real goldmine lies in maximizing the value you provide to your existing customers. Upselling and cross-selling are the secret weapons that empower you to do just that. By offering additional products or services that enhance the customer's purchase, you can not only increase their satisfaction but also boost your revenue and foster long-term loyalty.

Section 2: Understanding Customer Needs and Preferences

To excel in upselling and cross-selling, you must become a master of understanding your customers. Dive deep into their needs, preferences, and buying patterns. Conduct thorough market research, analyse customer data, and segment your customer base. This invaluable knowledge will enable you to identify opportunities for personalized recommendations and tailor your offers to provide maximum value.

Section 3: Crafting Irresistible Offers

Now comes the exciting part - crafting offers that customers simply can't resist. You're upselling and cross-selling offers should be carefully designed to align with the customer's journey and address their specific needs. Highlight the additional benefits, features, or cost savings they stand to gain by opting for the upgraded or complementary products. Paint a picture of how their experience will be elevated and how their goals will be achieved with these added enhancements.

Section 4: Effective Sales Techniques

To successfully execute upselling and cross-selling strategies, you need a well-trained and motivated sales team. Provide them with the tools, knowledge, and skills to identify opportunities, understand the customer's motivations, and effectively communicate the benefits of the additional products. Encourage a consultative selling approach, where your team acts as trusted advisors, offering personalized recommendations based on the customer's unique needs and aspirations.

Section 5: Integration into the Customer Experience

Seamless integration is the key to turning upselling and cross-selling into a natural part of the customer experience. Your website, e-commerce platform, or physical store should be designed to encourage exploration and discovery of additional options. Implement personalized product recommendations, bundle offers, and post-purchase follow-ups to engage customers and entice them to make additional purchases. Make it easy, convenient, and enjoyable for them to say "yes" to your upselling and cross-selling offers.

Key Takeaways:

1. Upselling and cross-selling are potent strategies that drive revenue, customer satisfaction, and loyalty.

2. Deeply understand your customers' needs and preferences to identify relevant upselling and cross-selling opportunities.

3. Craft compelling offers that highlight the added value and benefits of the additional products or services.

4. Empower your sales team with training and tools to effectively identify and communicate upselling and cross-selling opportunities.

5. Seamlessly integrate upselling and cross-selling into the customer experience, leveraging personalized recommendations, bundles, and follow-ups.

Action Points:

1. Conduct comprehensive market research and analyse customer data to uncover upselling and cross-selling opportunities within your customer base.

2. Develop targeted upselling and cross-selling offers that resonate with your customers' needs and desires.

3. Provide comprehensive sales training to your team, focusing on consultative selling techniques and effective communication of upselling and cross-selling offers.

4. Optimize your website or store layout to promote upselling and cross-selling opportunities, utilizing personalized product recommendations and enticing bundle offers.

5. Implement post-purchase follow-ups to remind customers of relevant upselling and cross-selling options, fostering repeat purchases and long-term customer relationships.

Having gained invaluable insights into the world of upselling and cross-selling. By understanding your customers, crafting irresistible offers, empowering your sales team, and integrating these strategies into the customer experience, you are poised for exponential business growth. Embrace the power of upselling and cross-selling, and watch your revenue soar as you create memorable experiences for your customers. Get ready to unlock your business's full potential!

CHAPTER 23

The Art of Customer Retention: Building Lasting Relationships

"*Customer satisfaction is worthless. Customer loyalty is priceless.*" - Jeffrey Gitomer

We now embark on a journey to master the art of customer retention. In the bustling world of business, acquiring new customers is only the first step. True success lies in your ability to forge deep and lasting connections with your existing customers. This chapter is dedicated to helping you cultivate strong relationships, foster loyalty, and propel your business towards exponential growth. So, let's dive in and discover the secrets of customer retention!

Section 1: Understanding the Value of Customer Retention

Picture this: a business that consistently retains its customers, enjoys their repeat business, and nurtures long-term relationships. This section emphasizes the immense value of customer retention. By focusing on keeping your existing customers happy and loyal, you can unlock the hidden potential of your business and drive long-term profitability.

Key Takeaway: Customer retention is not just a nice-to-have; it's a strategic imperative that fuels exponential growth and financial success.

Section 2: Creating a Customer-Centric Culture

At the heart of customer retention lies a customer-centric culture. This section explores the power of aligning your entire organization around the goal of delivering exceptional customer experiences. From the CEO to the frontline employees, everyone plays a crucial role in building and nurturing customer relationships.

Key Takeaway: Every member of your team should be an ambassador for customer-centricity, as customer loyalty begins with a collective commitment to exceptional service.

Section 3: Personalization and Customization

Customers today expect personalized experiences tailored to their unique preferences and needs. This section reveals the transformative impact of personalization and customization. We delve into techniques for collecting and utilizing customer data to create tailor-made products, services, and communications that resonate with individual customers.

Key Takeaway: By treating each customer as an individual and customizing your offerings, you can create a strong emotional connection that keeps them coming back.

Section 4: Building Trust and Loyalty

Trust is the cornerstone of enduring customer relationships. In this section, we explore strategies for building trust, including transparent communication, delivering on promises, and providing exceptional customer support. We also delve into the power of loyalty programs, rewards, and incentives in nurturing customer loyalty.

Key Takeaway: Building trust is an ongoing process that requires open communication, reliability, and a genuine desire to exceed customer expectations.

Section 5: Proactive Customer Engagement and Feedback

Don't wait for your customers to reach out to you—take the initiative to engage with them proactively. This section emphasizes the importance of staying connected and gathering feedback from your customers. We delve into techniques such as personalized communications, surveys, and social media listening, which empower you to understand your customers better and address their needs.

Key Takeaway:

Actively seek feedback, listen to your customers, and use their insights to continuously improve your products, services, and overall customer experience.

Section 6: Continual Improvement and Innovation

To retain customers in the long run, you must continually evolve and innovate. This section stresses the significance of staying ahead of market trends, anticipating customer needs, and continuously improving your offerings. By demonstrating a commitment to excellence and adaptability, you can inspire customer loyalty and differentiate yourself from competitors.

Key Takeaway: Embrace a mindset of continuous improvement, foster innovation within your organization, and stay one step ahead of your customers' evolving needs.

Action Points:

1. Evaluate your current customer retention strategies and metrics to identify areas for improvement.
2. Train and empower your team to prioritize customer-centricity and provide exceptional service at every customer touchpoint.
3. Implement personalized communication strategies, leveraging customer data to enhance the customer experience.
4. Develop and implement loyalty programs or incentives that reward customers for their continued support.
5. Regularly gather customer feedback, analyse it diligently, and take actionable steps to address any concerns or suggestions.

Remember, customer retention is not a passive endeavour but a strategic pursuit that demands your unwavering dedication. By cultivating a customer-centric culture, personalizing experiences, building trust, engaging proactively, and continuously innovating, you will lay a solid foundation for lasting customer relationships and exponential business growth. Take these lessons to heart and watch as your business thrives through the power of customer retention.